Soul Nutrition

DEBRA MCCURTAIN

BALBOA.PRESS
A DIVISION OF HAY HOUSE

Balboa Press books may be ordered through booksellers or by contacting:

Balboa Press
A Division of Hay House
1663 Liberty Drive
Bloomington, IN 47403
www.balboapress.com
1 (877) 407-4847

Because of the dynamic nature of the Internet, any web addresses or links contained in this book may have changed since publication and may no longer be valid. The views expressed in this work are solely those of the author and do not necessarily reflect the views of the publisher, and the publisher hereby disclaims any responsibility for them.

The author of this book does not dispense medical advice or prescribe the use of any technique as a form of treatment for physical, emotional, or medical problems without the advice of a physician, either directly or indirectly. The intent of the author is only to offer information of a general nature to help you in your quest for emotional and spiritual well-being. In the event you use any of the information in this book for yourself, which is your constitutional right, the author and the publisher assume no responsibility for your actions.

Any people depicted in stock imagery provided by Getty Images are models, and such images are being used for illustrative purposes only. Certain stock imagery © Getty Images.

Print information available on the last page.

ISBN: 978-1-9822-3850-6 (sc)
ISBN: 978-1-9822-3851-3 (e)

Balboa Press rev. date: 11/19/2019

Dedicated to my soul

Where I discovered the barriers to my heart.

Shed myself of

False beliefs.

Religion.

Incest

Shame

Guilt

Rage

Fear

Hatred

To Ancestors

To Angels

To Spirit Guides

To The Divine Feminine

To All That Is

To The Wellness Institute

To the Universe

To my Soul

To the Great Spirit

To Cala

To Josh

To Goldie

I AM FEARLESS

AHO

CONTENTS

1   The Peace Practice.. 1

2   Heart Centered Hypnotherapy...................................... 13

3   Integration 21

4   The Fire of Transformation 33

INTRODUCTION

The two words Soul Nutrition began to become the rhythm of my heartbeat a year ago. I heard them in my head. Felt them inside of me. Saw them everywhere. These two words had presence. They were so strong like a vision. I knew the direction I was headed in. A weight loss healing practice. The universe was turning my head around again. I was fearful. What? How? Why? When? I had started a weight loss corporation that was very successful nine years ago. Based on a diet pill. At first it was all I knew. I had come from a very large weight loss practice. It was how they did it. It was good enough until it wasn't. Then another door opened. The soul highway. The journey to my heart center. My soul. My essence. Journaling. Meditating. Breathing. Yoga. Healing. Whatever I was curious about I tried. Discovered things about myself along the way. That I was unhappy and stressed out. Realized that I was just like my clients who were obsessed with their weight. The scale. The restrictions. The control. The binging. The cleanliness of my home. All were symbolic of shame. Memories that were buried so deep within my subconscious that it took fifty seven years and a miracle to face. To heal and to have compassion for myself. The Universe became my teacher. My soul the playground. I separated myself for a bit from all that was familiar to heal myself. I am becoming whole. I am a child of the universe. I began to learn a new language. The language of love and the ancient wisdom of healing. Meditation. Chakras. Reiki. Hypnotherapy. Soul Retrieval. Breath-work. Sleeping to the lullaby of Hindu Chanting. Universal Energy. Rumi. Subtle Energy. I am a student of all of them. At my core is light. The power to heal. I cultivate my gifts and am honored to share them. The curtain of conflict has fallen. The conversations with clients about weight loss has completely changed from restrictive dieting to compassion. From judgement to grace. From self hate to trust and love. I shifted my weight loss practice to embrace the principles of soul nutrition: self love and hypnotherapy. I am a guide to the doorway of the soul. To all that is and ever was and ever will be. This work is profound. I am powered by the Great Spirit. The core emotions of shame and fear leave an indelible mark on the soul. My job is to retrieve the soul back into the body and set that bitch on fire. It is my truth. It is why I came. Soul Nutrition. My time is now. From my heart to yours. Namaste.

ONE

THE PEACE PRACTICE

You are not defined by the scale. Happiness is a skill. You are a miracle. Make no mistake about it. If you fight a war with food everyday then this book is for you. If you wake up every morning, get on the scale and wish less for your body this book is for you. If you look in the mirror and see imperfection in your soul this book is for you. If your life is defined by the latest fad diet this book is for you. If you restrict yourself with food, binge and purge then this book is for you. If you have lost the ability to trust yourself with food then this book is for you. If you disassociate from your body during the day because of the incredible demands of work and family, not eating until you return home then binging for hours then this book is for you. If you still remember the moment when your mother called you fat then this book is for you. If your inner child needs a soul retrieval because of trauma then this book is for you. If those words and those memories have left a mark on your soul that no diet or pill or cleanse or binge or drug can make you whole again then this book is for you. Got it? Good. I am in the weight loss world. I have been here for the past fifteen years. It has been the wildest ride ever. I am the CEO of Soul Nutrition. A holistic weight loss practice based on nourishment of the soul: hypnotherapy, intuitive eating, juice cleansing and cosmic coaching. I still have one foot in the medical weight loss world but in my heart is this holistic weight loss practice. Make no mistake about it, medical weight loss is a thirty billion dollar industry based on fear and false beliefs about women. I have learned that eating disorders have roots in trauma. If you can control the scale you can control the trauma. I learned that I was no different than any woman who walked through my doors. I am obsessed with my weight. Spent most of my life disassociated from my body. Had my first eating disorder at the age of thirteen. A repressed memory of sexual abuse at the age of 57. My relationship with everything was about trauma control. I purge no more. The journey of self discovery taught me that. My intuition and my heart center are in the drivers seat. I eat when I am hungry and stop when I am satisfied. My weight is magical now. I love my body. Nourishment of my soul is the highway I follow. I am whole. I am safe. I am in my body. I matter. I am fearless. I am worthy of living a live full of joy and magic.

It all goes down as Self Discovery. The moment when you come face to face with your soul. The doorway opens and you have two choices. Love or fear. It is in every beat of your heart and every whisper of your soul, your spirit, your essence, your truth. When you step into your soul, magic happens. You become a force to be reckoned with. You stand in starlight. Your heart is the intersection between the soul and all that is. Connect to it. Honor every emotion. Every feeling. Every tear. Every fear. Release. Breathe. Stand tall. Show up and stay present. It all starts in the morning where you begin to create an emotional bridge between your mind and your soul.

Be fearless with yourself. Walk a different path. The path of conscious awareness. I am going to teach you the soul highway. It begins with a peace practice. AHO.

> The morning breeze has secrets to tell You. Do not go back to sleep.
> –Rumi

The time to stop fighting a war with yourself everyday is now. Lay down the sword. Give yourself permission. It will be okay. You are safe. Before I will even mention food and trust me this is what I do all day long, the first step in healthy body weight is the peace practice. Let's walk the soul highway together. What is your self care practice? Do you have one? You cannot nourish your body with healthy food if you aren't nourishing your soul with love. The two go hand in hand. It all goes down in the morning. Get up earlier. Rumi is a twelfth century Persian poet and he has many quotes about love and the heart. Thousands of years later his words breathe life into many souls. Get up earlier and take a deep breath. Honor yourself. You are part of a planet, YES I SAID PLANET, the latest estimates are that earth is 4.54 billion years old. You are a part of that. A place where civilizations and species have come and gone. Our existence is **Sacred. Our planet stardust.** It has left us wisdom and great beauty that is waiting and the only requirement is connection. So connect. Journal. Meditate. Get a cup of coffee and go sit outside. Pay attention to the downloads of the universe. Transform. Set your soul on fire. Love yourself. Slow the fuck down. Send gratitude and love to yourself and this planet earth by saying thank you for yet another opportunity on this amazing planet that is traveling 1000 mph as it rotates around the Sun. We are stardust. You are a miracle. Your most important relationship is the one with yourself. The morning. The morning. The morning. Let no tasks enter your mind. Spend thirty minutes or an hour where you do you. Don't run away from yourself. Bust out a journal. This is my cheap notebook theory of life. Or a candle or music or a book. Send your body and mind love. Look at your body in the mirror and come home. Repeat after me. I am a miracle. I am beautiful. I love myself.

Believe me you need healing. We all do. Stop denying that everything in your life is fine. It isn't and that is okay because the time to stand in your power is right now. To face yourself with grace. Beauty and joy awaits.

Fear and anxiety will fade. What is inside of you is waiting for you to wake up and take your first breath. Let's take that first breath of your soul. Your spirit. We are going to build a platform for self love. No one teaches us this shit when we are young. I stumbled upon it later in life. Glad I did. It is a everyday practice for the rest of your life. Stay Connected.

Stop running away from yourself. I will repeat this over and over again. You are meant for grace, beauty and wonder. You are a miracle. You are here in this lifetime for a reason and it isn't your weight. It is your truth. Your gifts. What brings you joy. Your soul light. Your heart. Not in the physical sense. Not the pump. Your heart is the core of your emotional and spiritual being. It is the seat of your soul. It is the intersection of your essence. The ability to feel love for yourself and others. To laugh spontaneously. To love unconditionally. To be. To feel something. To feel compassion. To be touched. Made love to. To be able to let go of what no longer serves your highest good. To comfort yourself. To forgive. To take the time to discover why you are here. What is your truth? Create your peace practice and make it your own. When I first got started I journaled. If journaling isn't your thing fine. Find what works and practice it everyday.

JOURNALING PARAGRAPH ONE: THE DREAM STATE

Your dreams are a window to the soul. A doorway to your subconscious mind. They hold keys to the past and present. Conflict is brought to the surface during the dream state. We have access to those conflicts when the veil of the ego is dropped during sleep. Pay attention to them. They are symbolic. The soul can travel to other realms. You can have out of body experiences. There are many dimensions to this world. Have fun. Write it down. Journal first thing in the morning. Because you will forget your dreams. Whatever you can remember write it down. Books have been written on this subject. Don't dismiss your dreams. If you can't remember your dream don't sweat it.

JOURNALING PARAGRAPH TWO: GRATITUDE

The second paragraph is what you are thankful for. This affirms the good. Every moment there are lessons to be learned about ourselves. Be grateful for this and all things no matter how difficult. There should be at least three things you are grateful for. Can be more. Go back and read this part of your journaling six months down the road. Your emotional growth will surprise you. Nuff said.

JOURNALING PARAGRAPH THREE: CONSCIOUS MIND

The third paragraph is where the magic happens. What is going on in the beautiful mind of yours in the morning? What is that thread of thought? Write it down. Get it out. Remember that this is your private journal. If someone happens to pick it up and start reading it that is on them. I used to hide my journal then I thought "What am I hiding? My true self? Nah." Be an open book. Unlock your secrets. Figure out the frequency of your journaling. It's your pacing. Just do it. You will feel better when you journal. It's emotional release plain and simple. It is the path to self healing.

I N S P I R A T I O N

You aren't done yet. Find an affirmation each day that speaks to you! Or start a vision board. This gets whatever your vision is for yourself out of your head and makes it real. Gives it life. It is emotional validation. Soul motivation. In case you haven't noticed this inspiration stuff is a movement right now. Pinterest is a great source for vision boards. Stay inspired. My earliest affirmation that I revisit is," Everyday we have two choices love or fear". Followed by I am Beautiful. I am worthy. I am starlight. I am a miracle. I am worthy. I am a bad ass. I am the Divine Feminine.

SOUL HIGHWAY

So you've created space in the morning. Greeted the day. Journaled. This platform is deep and wide and it is yours to create. We are not finished with the peace practice of honoring yourself in the morning. Meditation is next. Yes I said it. Meditation. Before you dismiss the idea hold up, breathe and hear me out. Meditation is the way. It is **SACRED.** I used to be a type A personality. I was defined by the tasks that I completed. It started in the morning. I got up with my hair on fire. First I would put a load of laundry in the washer. Empty the dishwasher. Start breakfast for the kids. Clean up the kitchen. Skip breakfast. I couldn't breathe. I owned a business, had employees, a husband, two kids. I enjoyed none of it. I went from one task to the next. Disconnected. Miserable. I drank wine to numb myself. Mercy fucked my husband. One spring morning on a vacation with my husband in Scott's Valley, California my whole life changed. It began with an argument about the direction of the morning. He wanted to go hiking. I wanted to go to the beach. We got into it over something so simple. He stormed off to take a shower and I sat on the bed wondering what had just happened?

I turned on the television and it was on the public broadcasting station. There was Wayne Dyer with a beret on his head and a children's choir behind him. He was talking about his book, "The Power of Intention". That our thoughts are powerful. Wanting more for others than we want for ourselves. Compassion. Connection to the power of this ancient universe that has secrets to tell us about joy, love, forgiveness. Clues to why we are here. That the connection is meditation. Being still with ourselves long enough to listen to our soul, our hearts that always know the way when we are lost. He was talking about self discovery. That what is inside is more important that what is outside. That our ego gets in the way of our truth. Happiness. Joy. I needed to hear that. That moment my life as I knew it changed. His words were like fire that ignited my soul. I began to learn a different language. The language of love. Of Grace and compassion. I let go of my ego: that little voice of conflict and negativity that told me I wasn't good enough to live a life of joy. That I was worthless and ugly. That I would never be successful. Happy. That I was fat. That nobody loved me. That I really didn't know what love is. That fear was my constant companion. I took my first spiritual breath. The universe turned my head 360 degrees towards my soul. I started journaling and meditating. I unraveled myself. Happiness is a skill and when I unraveled myself to the core and discovered the deep shame that lied there I had a soft place to land. Thank you Wayne Dyer. Thank you.

SIT WITH YOURSELF AND BREATHE

Remember that it all goes down in the morning. Self love. Whatever resistance you have to meditation let it go and do it everyday for at least five minutes for the rest of your life. **THIS IS A SACRED GIFT OF CONNECTION TO ALL THAT IS AND EVER WILL BE.** If life isn't working right now the doorway is beginning to open. The doorway to why you are really here on this planet. To love and to be loved. To be healed. To heal others. I used to think that all this stuff was bullshit. Living your best life. Finding your joy and happiness, And it found me. All you have to do is show up everyday for yourself. You are an energy body and your energy body needs work. It is time for alignment. Stay with me. Your energy body is your soul. Spirit. It is your joy. Your light. Your essence. Your heart. There is a belief that we come from the spirit world into our physical bodies for a reason. That we come with purpose. That purpose is love. Self love and anything that get's in the way of that needs change. Get your spirit armour on. Because we reside in the physical world where false beliefs are everywhere. Where we have been taught that we are defined by perfection and material possessions. It's an illusion. Fulfillment has nothing to do with this. Get off the wheel.

Connect to your soul. Walk the soul highway. Let's begin connecting to all that is. Connect. Listen. Learn. Let go. Change. Have compassion for yourself. Live. Love. Don't overthink meditation.

GO SIT SOMEWHERE OR LIE DOWN

Anywhere is fine. Inside or out. Go to your place of power wherever that is. I go outside because nature has secrets to tell. Sit or lie flat. Floor or chair. No judgement. Pick your spot. Sit down. For five minutes and breathe. Take deep breaths in and exhale. Some breathe in through the nose and out through the nose or mouth. Your choice. Just breathe. If thoughts appear let them pass and focus on your breathing. I use an app called Insight Timer. There are meditation masters there. YouTube is another source. Again your choice. You don't need them. I stumbled upon Insight Timer it's for free and the meditations changed my life because they opened the doorway to my soul and brought each barrier that surrounded my heart to my conscious mind for healing. With each barrier that was healed tremendous light followed. I was able to make more space for good in my life. In short meditation is a miracle. Make this a daily practice. Morning or evening your pick. Just sit with yourself and breathe. You will connect to the source that made all that is. It is the foundation of the soul highway. The Divine Feminine. Your essence. Why you came. Start walking it. Keep walking it. Stay connected.

T H E   H E A R T

> Your task is not to seek for love, but merely to seek and find all the barriers within yourself that you have built against it
> –Rumi

Once you are finished with the session pay attention to the shift in energy and the message from above. My Anam Cara refers to this as the downloads. The straight up consciousness stream that has information for you. Write that shit down! Or if a person comes to mind that you need to forgive or something that needs to be let go of. Listen. Walk in it. Feel it. Bring it into your soul. Your heart knows the way. Some cultures refer to the heart as the seat of the soul. It is virtuous and precious. It is a trip literally. It's like learning a new language. The language of love. At first it might be awkward. Uncomfortable. Different. Unsteady. Move past your fear and connect again and again and again. Never stop. The first time I meditated I didn't like it. It felt uncomfortable. My mind that had a million things going on inside of it was blank after my first session. I wasn't sure if this was for me but tried it again and that is where the magic happened. I lost track of time during my second session. Five minutes turned into ten. It felt great. There was a sense of renewal. I came back into my home ready to get all of the endless tasks done and a voice without sound stated," Get back outside.". I grabbed my dogs leashes and went on a long walk. That was **THE LAST DAY THAT I WASTED LIVING ON THIS EARTH.** I stopped being defined by the tasks that I completed. There is incredible beauty in moments. The work could wait. That feeling of joy I began to pay attention to.

It was profound. I wanted more of it. A lot more. There was a quiet presence inside of me. Something strong. Wise. It was and still is very very cool. It is my soul. I began to reclaim it.

Reclaim yours. You never know where you are going to wind up. But you will begin to notice your energy. Your soul. Your heart. It's gentleness. It's presence. It's whispers. It's truth. This is beautiful. When we are frightened of what we don't understand meditation can be a difficult proposition. I gave it a shot. And kept giving it a shot. It changed my whole world for the better. I began to connect to my heart. What held space inside of me. One by one the barriers to self love fell.

Lessons presented themselves. Things that I needed to work through that got in the way of my essence. My beauty. My truth. This takes time so be patient. And stick with your awareness of yourself. Don't run away from anything anymore. What holds negative space inside of you deal with. When you meditate ask for the next step. Feelings are okay. This work will create ripples in your world. Self love is worth every emotion. If I can do it. Anyone can. You can heal yourself with meditation. Plain and simple and get on with the business of living. Let go of what no longer serves your highest good. Don't get me wrong. Life is not a series of unicorns and rainbows it can be messy and shitty but those states can lead to change if you have the courage to open that doorway. That is where the magic happens. Meditation is self awareness. Self awareness is the work of the soul. Don't let anything or anyone get between you and your soul light. **I am going to get right to it.** The obsession with your weight is about trauma control. If you can control your weight you can control the memory whether subconscious or conscious of trauma. When someone took a part of your soul. I came face to face with mine one morning in February of 2018. Get some tissue and sit down. It's gonna hurt.

D O I N G   T H E   W O R K

Most of us who are living and breathing on this planet have experienced trauma. My childhood I survived. But the subconscious mind is an interesting thing. It hides what we are not ready to see. Masks itself in addictions or eating disorders. One morning the veil was lifted. My three year old had the courage to show up. She needed healing. It was a morning in February of 2018. I woke up. Had coffee. Meditated. Then I came face to face with a memory that I had spent a lifetime repressing. That I was raped when I was three years old. It was brought straight to my conscious mind. I was right there. I saw everything. The house on Douglas Road. The room. Sitting on the bed. The dress I had on. The white lace socks. The black dress shoes. The roses that were on the comforter covering the bed. A part of my soul left my body that day. Everything that I had ever known to be true about myself shattered. My whole life made sense that morning. Fear. Doubt. Shame. Rage. There was terror in my soul. I fell so hard and so fast that morning and the universe held me in it's soul light. It took my heart and wrapped it in stardust. It kissed my soul while opening up the doorway to shame and fear. The practice of self peace that I had built held me. It brought healers one by one so that I could retrieve pieces of my soul and bring them back home. I wanted to crawl into a hole and die that morning but my truth was arriving. The core of my being presented. Why I am here. Why I am in the weight loss world.

TWO

HEART CENTERED HYPNOTHERAPY

I have since learned that I am a miracle. I am a survivor. That trauma can be separated from sex. I am beauty. I am light. I am love. I am worthy of joy. My body is beautiful. I began to shed myself that day. I became vulnerable. I shook from the inside out for months but I kept showing up for myself and journaling, meditating and breathing. My energy body was emerging. I began to do Chakra work. I see color when I meditate. It's the Chakras. The root chakra work was just beginning. I began to explore ancient healing traditions like Reiki and Shamanism. I became a healer that day. It takes courage, self love and compassion. I am not defined by incest. It is just a chapter in the book of Debra McCurtain. I am healed by the sacred divine for the benefit of all the sacred divine. This is a beautiful gift. I am learning compassion, patience and self love. Gratitude for being alive on this beautiful planet. Having the courage to dream and have vision. To deepen my spiritual practice. When I turn fifty nine later this year I am going to go on a Vision Quest in the mountains of Utah. Something I have always wanted to do. I have courage now. I have let go of fear and doubt. The work is ongoing. Those around me either get on board or get gone. I am not fucking around with my life anymore. I encourage my client's to do the same. Figure it out. Take chances. Love yourself through everything. Doing the work included hypnotherapy. This is why I came.

You can't take clients places you haven't been. The correlation between the obsession with weight loss and trauma presented itself. It was a truth. I figured out my role quickly. That of a hypnotherapist. My therapist performed hypnotherapy on me. It was a profound experience. I was able to begin healing my soul. She performed a soul retrieval where I was able to resource myself and integrate my heart back into my soul that had been lost for fifty four years. I was healed by the sacred divine for the benefit of all the sacred divine. Clients showed up telling me their stories. I was ready to hear it. All this time this is was what weight loss was really about. Trauma control pound for pound.

It is about trauma, soul retrieval and the healing of the inner child. One. Two. Three. The inability to lose weight is the inner child who lost a part of their soul that is waiting to come home. Still terrified of showing themselves. Hiding. The cycle of emotional eating is symbolic of the three year old who wants what they want when they want it. The six year old who feels invisible. Or the nine year old that simply split. They never leave us. The seven year old who doesn't want to draw attention to herself because it comes with a price. Hypnotherapy acknowledges these little ones. Gives them a voice. Retrieves their souls and brings them home to the heart. The adult can become whole and disassociate less when triggered at home or at work or both. A healthy relationship with food is not possible unless this work is started. All of those little memories that float in and out of your conscious mind that you tell yourself are okay aren't. It's a part of your soul that is calling. I have a teddy bear that I sleep with and she is my three year old. I am good to her. I love her. I protect her. I see her. She will always be with me but now I know what she needs and I am aware. I keep her safe. Unless the healing work is done weight loss is an illusion and an unattainable one. Being able to nourish your body and mind is not possible. **DO THE WORK. KEEP DOING THE WORK.** There isn't one client who walks through my door who doesn't have an eating disorder large or small.

I verbalize this with clients first. Then I begin to unravel the soul with grace and love during hypnotherapy and bring it home to the heart cleansed and sacred again. My three year old lost her heart on that bed. With my spirit guide and spirit animal retrieved it during hypnotherapy. Cleansed it from shame and fear and put it back into my body where it belonged. Bringing it home felt sacred. The obsession with the scale may never go away and actually I don't own a scale now but healing the inside wounds will give the scale less power and a healthy relationship with food is possible along with the most powerful medicine on the planet **SELF LOVE and hypnotherapy.** Stay with me. Stay with yourself. Clients are able to go deep into the subconscious and see where they made decisions and conclusions based on trauma. Spin it. Heal it. Begin to practice self love. Weight loss begins on the inside. I never have to do to much convincing about the need for hypnotherapy. The two words that work like magic are inner child and soul retrieval. Usually weight loss follows after one session but more important they are able to smile, have compassion for themselves and begin to heal. To live lives of joy and peace. I love that.

It isn't about weight loss. It is about letting go of the obsession with losing weight. Letting go of restricting yourself with food. Not letting the scale define you and to take away your soul. It's about sending your body love. It's about having compassion for yourself. Breathing. Falling in love with the fact that you are a miracle. Your body is beautiful. You are amazing. You came from love. You are love. You are worthy of joy and magic. Believe in yourself. Begin to embrace the concept of nourishment. Your most important relationship is the one with yourself. I am going to make an argument for the necessity for heart centered hypnotherapy as a platform for weight loss. Weight loss begins on the inside.

There are common misconceptions about hypnotherapy that I spend a short time dispelling. That you will cluck like chicken. Not true. That you aren't in control. Not true. That it's mind control. Not true. Here's the quick and dirty. The whole process takes 60-90 minutes depending on the skill level of the practitioner. Sessions start with an interview. I let the client know that they are always in control and if at any time during the session they want to stop all they have to do is raise their hand and let me know. I also let them know that they are not alone and that I am with them. The interview takes 10-15 minutes. I get the client comfortable and begin to ask them what they want to work on or why they are here. It's usually weight loss related with my clients but I did have a client who wanted to work on a particular person who kept appearing in her dreams that she did not know in this lifetime. I did Subtle Energy stuff on her which was cool. With the assistance of St. Michael wrapped that lost soul in a net of white light while she cut chords. Back to the interview. Once the conflict is identified next core emotion are revealed. What is the emotion underneath the conflict. Is it anger, shame, fear, sadness, guilt? It is located it in the body whether chest, head, belly, heart. Then the severity of the emotion is rated on a scale of 1-10. The goal is to move the emotion out of the body. Give it a voice. To release emotional weight.

The next step is the hypnotic state which is a natural one. It is the pre sleep state where the ego has fallen and the subconscious mind is accessed. This is where all memories are stored like a super computer. Accessing it is key to hypnotherapy. The hypnotherapist is mirror of your soul.

It takes about fifteen to twenty minutes to get to the place where the doorway to the subconscious mind is opened. I use music that the client prefers and it is a gentle guided muscular progressive relaxation from head to toe coupled with breathing. Inhaling the intention of peace and exhaling what no longer serves your highest good. I love this process. I use an elevator after this with ten floors of progressive relaxation. If the client is into chakras I use them as well

Anchoring the positive aspects of the self comes next. Anchors are identified by the client as their favorite place, spiritual connection and wise adult. These are important prior to accessing the subconscious mind. Remember the subconscious arena is uncharted territory and often times what is seen there can be shocking but necessary. This is where the healing occurs. It is a beautiful process that flows. It is a natural process as well. Nothing is forced.

S T A T E   O F   G R A C E

Then the work begins. It's important to track the client. Not lead them. The client enters a state of grace with themselves. Taking the core emotion identified early on and releasing it from the body. Giving the body part a voice. Speaking directly to the person involved. Saying what they want to say. Capturing a part of the soul that was lost during a traumatic event that the subconscious mind has pushed down within the deeper recesses for protection. I encourage the client to stay with themselves here. Age regression occurs as the pattern of the core emotion is revealed for clarity and the emotional bridge between the adult conflict and the inner child trauma is made. Soul retrieval's occur with each hypnotherapy session I perform and are common place amongst other hypnotherapists. The client does the work of retrieving the lost soul piece or pieces often with their spiritual connection. Through my Shamanic training I am able only as a last resort to go into the traumatic event with the client and retrieve the lost soul piece. Cleansing it of what no longer serves the clients highest good. I am always profoundly touched during the cleansing process. How beautiful it is. How innocence is cleansed of shame by their spiritual connection God or St. Michael and it shines with light. I can see what they see. With their hands bringing it back into their heart. I feel as if we are in a state of grace and we certainly are. I have subtle energy training. Before I zip up the clients energy field or lock in the new soul pieces I ask them to locate any areas of heaviness. This is an organic process as they always

17

know where these areas are. They began pulling out this energy chord that contains negative energy that is attached to someone that they know. This chord needs to be pulled and the person on the other end identified. Once the chord is pulled out it is cut by snapping the fingers or using gold scissors. The clients always feels lighter after this. Then the soul pieces that have come home are locked in.

The client then dialogues with the inner child. Begins to heal that young soul with words. This is so profound a process. So loving. New affirmations are made by the client and these are written down. Processing the session is next. It takes the client a bit of time here. They have spent an hour or so deep within the recesses of their mind and body that integrating back to the now requires a shift in consciousness. Water is necessary and the time to ground themselves. They get it. I review the behaviors with food and connection with the healing of the inner child. They get it. Then they work on dialoging with that inner child on a consistent basis so that that part of them feels safe enough to embrace the concept of nourishment. To make better choices with food. I usually give them meditation homework involving the Root Chakra which is safety and security based. Client's are always blown away and profoundly grateful. I have heard this statement a million times, "I never thought it was going to go like this today followed by thank you". Hypnotherapy is a tremendous healing modality also known as a miracle. Weight loss is symbolic of the healing of the inner child. Get to it. Your soul will thank you. You will begin to walk in this world a different way. The way of the spirit. Your consciousness will expand. Your heart will grow. You will have more compassion for yourself. The doorway to your soul will open. Your behaviors with food whether you restrict or binge and purge or all three will subside. You will begin to give yourself permission to nourish yourself from the inside out. I have incorporated hypnotherapy into my weight loss practice and shifted from medical weight loss to a holistic one. It is in my soul. It is why I came.

CLEINT PRESENTATION

All hypnotherapy visits are profound. I will present this one. The client was male. His presenting conflict was his weight. Specifically belly fat. He was very happy in all areas of his life except for his weight. He fought a war with it everyday. The core emotion that he identified was shame and sadness. It was located in his belly. The induction into the deep relaxation phase went smooth. Anchors were identified. The age regression piece of this session along with the soul retrieval that followed were profound. I use this word a lot when discussing hypnotherapy. He age regressed to the age of nine, following the thread of the core emotion identified as shame and sadness as it relates to his weight. At the age of nine he immigrated to America from the Middle East. He was at the airport with his family and his father was unable to complete the journey. His visa wasn't granted. He had to say goodbye. Part of his soul split and went with his father. He remembered seeing part of him leave his body and take his father's hand and the other part went with his mother. He concluded in that airport that he wanted everyone to be together and that he had to grow up fast. He decided that he was to take care of his mom and that he was responsible for his mother and father's happiness. He began to gain weight right after this. Ninety pounds to be exact. The soul retrieval was to merge both parts of his soul. He was able to coax the nine year old away from his father's hands by holding out his hands and embracing him. Before the souls could be merged they needed to be cleansed of guilt as the children felt responsible for the father and mother's happiness. Keep in mind that the client does all the work. The souls were merged and the client cried and cried. He brought the nine year old home into his heart. I take time here.

Before his energy field was closed with this new soul piece by myself energetically I wanted to cut any negative energy chords from his body that were participating in a negative feedback loop. I have been trained in Subtle

Energy technique and I use it with each session. This is the fascinating part. He identified an area of heaviness in his body which was his belly. He pulled this chord away from his body like a rope. He pulled and pulled and felt it in his back. It was a very heavy chord. When I asked him who or what was it attached to he stated, "It's my belly fat". Then I asked him," What is the belly fat symbolic of?" He replied, "It's the weight of the nine year old part of me that left and stayed behind with my dad". He then cut this chord by snapping his fingers some use golden scissors. I was amazed as was he. His new conclusions were that he was going to be more carefree. That he deserved to be happy. That he mattered. That he would spend more time having fun. That he wasn't responsible for everyone. He dialogued with his inner child that was nine. Told him he was beautiful and deserved to be happy. This is such a sacred process of healing the inner child. After the session he spoke of that day as a nine year old and how he had never forgotten it. He was surprised about the belly fat and what it signified. He was blown away by the soul retrieval. I encouraged him to go slow and integrate the nine year old. That the nine year old needed healing. To dialogue with him. That his weight loss struggles were about him. He made that emotional bridge connection. That fun was medicine in his world. To have much more of it. Such a great session and I will never forget it and was then as now honored to be a part of it.

I believe four things actually five things to be true about weight loss. One is hypnotherapy because weight loss begins on the inside. Two is intuitive eating as it is absolute genius. Let the mind and body do the work. Three is gut health as our gut is our second brain. I am always amazed at how little humans know about their own bodies. Knowledge is power but also requires the next step which is what are you going to do with it otherwise it is just a thought. The fourth principle is exercise. The fifth meal planning.

THREE

I N T E G R A T I O N

Now we can talk about food. Nourishment is a process. A concept. It is the integration of the mind, body and soul. What you allow and what you let go of. What brings you joy and strength. It is clarity. It is self love. With hypnotherapy you can begin to lose emotional weight which makes space for giving yourself the permission to nourish your body, mind and soul. To see what the behaviors with food are really about. Trauma control. To let go of the obsession with food and the scale. I believe in Intuitive Eating and Intermittent Fasting. Here it goes. Don't pay attention to the clock. Eat when you are hungry and stop when you are satisfied. This is my best advice. Each and every time that you have food in your mouth **ENGAGE YOUR BRAIN. Ask yourself three questions: 1- How does this food taste in my mouth? 2- How do I feel about it? 3- Am I satisfied right now?** I have lost thirty pounds. Kept it off. Binged. Monitor my weight closely. I can honestly admit that I did not engage my brain when I had food in my mouth. I do now. Intuitive eating is what it is called and it is **genius.** Most of us disassociate during the day and certainly when we eat. Simply put we are outside of our bodies. We check out because of the tremendous demands of the day. Work. Family. Time. Getting the kids to school.

Juggling sports schedules. It never ends. Food is a side note. Hastily planned. We choke it down fast and move onto the next task. I learned about disassociation during hypnotherapy training. It made sense. Then the correlation was made during conversations with women who went all day without eating and when they returned home from work or when the kids finally went to sleep then binged because they returned to their bodies and felt hunger.

In some cultures food is an experience. Something to be honored for all of the work that is put into it. How it is grown. The soil it inhabits. The hands that have touched it. The process that got it to the table. That it actually has presence. We are what we eat. In the American culture for the most part it is a grab and go concept. A hurried one. The unhealthier the better. Don't get me started on the large portions that are also a staple of our society. Sugar is outlandish. Our bodies are perfect machines. On a cellular level the repair work is nonstop. Be good to your body mind and soul. Give your body what it needs so that it can do it's best for you. I promote nourishment and Intuitive Eating. Nourishment of the soul people! Stop dieting. **Intuitive eating** is a stretch for those of us who chronically diet and are obsessed with the scale. Restrict ourselves with food. Binge. Feel guilty. Get up and do it all over again. Trust me. I am in this category but I am better than I used to be. Intuitive eating has allowed me such freedom from dieting that I absolutely promote it and practice it. I have recently lost ten pounds doing it without the intention of losing weight. It has afforded me portion control. I engage my brain when I have food in my mouth. This engages my stomach which signals when I am satisfied and I choose to honor it's signal. I am able to portion control. I feel great. Eating is intuitive and mental. We all know what foods work for us and what foods don't. It's a conscious choice to honor that. If the intention is weight loss then the intention is weight loss. I don't believe it's healthy to want to lose weight then sabotage yourself. Which lead to feelings of guilt. It's a cycle that keeps repeating itself until you choose to stop being co dependent with yourself. Listen to your intuition. If you aren't a breakfast person don't eat it! Listen to your body. It isn't the most important meal of the day. Intermittent fasting has taught us that. For me it is healthy for the body to fast 16 hours in between dinner and the next meal. The reasons for this are complex but simply put our food supply has changed dramatically and an already stressed body has to work hard to break down food into macronutrients (protein, carbohydrates and fat) for energy. With this is a spike in blood sugar which requires the pancreas to release insulin to reduce the blood sugar. If blood sugar levels aren't normalized due to poor food choices then the body stores fat around the belly. This is a normal metabolic process that occurs when we eat. There is the concept of inflammation that is the outlier. I believe that this process of how our food is broken down for energy should be honored. The body works hard to convert food into energy which is what a calorie is. A calorie is a unit of heat that is converted into energy derived from food. Make it count. If you aren't a breakfast person then don't eat breakfast. Listen to your body's natural feeding rhythms. Don't ignore hunger signals. Plan for nourishment of your body. Figure out what foods give you energy and sound good and feel good to you. Eat. Check in with your brain and your gut. Begin to flow with food. Honor yourself with food. Connect to your body and mind. Say it with me, "You are worthy of nourishing your body with good food".

INFLAMMATION

Gut health cannot be emphasized enough. It is our second brain. It is as important if not more important than anything that you currently do to maintain your health and welfare. Research now indicates that gut health is linked to Alzheimer's. Imagine that. We know that the health of our gut indicates the health of our bodies in a much more serious way than ever imagined. The gut pulls nutrients out of our food for cellular energy. It is responsible for our immune function. Serotonin is synthesized there as well. The body is a perfect machine. It's always wanted to heal and repair itself. Gut health is a daily practice. When the belly is bloated the body is in an inflammatory state from the brain to the heart and all cells in between. Pay attention when your belly is bloated or you feel a heaviness in your belly. Ask yourself what did I just eat? Was it sugar? White flour products like pasta, bread? Fried something? Cheese? Stay away from it. Here's my speech to client's. Your belly is a biome. It is a living organism. It has a trillion fungus, yeast and bacterial cells. This is the interplay of gut health. It's all about balance. Important stuff right? We know what the gut likes and what it doesn't like. The concept is to keep it healthy on a daily basis to reduce inflammation in the body that leads to disease. It likes things that are fermented which is the breakdown of it's own composition: bacteria, fungus and yeast. This is so simple. It likes: Probiotics (bacteria), Kombucha (fermented tea) and Apple Cider Vinegar (fermented apple juice) and Kimchi (fermented vegetables). It doesn't like white flour products, gluten which is in wheat flour or sugar. Remember it is the balance of yeast, bacteria and fungus that is important. Anything that upsets this needs to be reduced in your diet. Keeping it healthy is the key. I take a probiotic everyday. Don't overthink probiotics. Don't spend a bunch of money. Find one that fits your lifestyle an works for you. How you know it's right is that your stools are regular and you have energy and a healthy immune system. I also consume apple cider vinegar everyday prior to lunch. I love Bragg's Apple Cider Vinegar. I dig Dr. Bragg's. Love her hat and love her message. I consider apple cider vinegar to be an old remedy. I started drinking it three years ago. My belly flattened out. I had more energy and I haven't been sick since. Not one cold or sniffle. It definitely decreased yeast in my body and increased the acidity level. The benefits are well documented. I am intuitive and gauge supplements by how I feel. I feel amazing on this stuff. Don't shoot it. I can't imagine how this administration process ever got started. But it has. So brutal on your upper stomach. Here is why. Your upper stomach is highly acidic to break down food contents for processing throughout the GI tract. It can dissolve a nail. Putting another substance into it that is also highly acidic is not a great idea. Client's always report that they hated taking apple cider vinegar which led to a conversation about how I take it. I put a tablespoon of apple cider vinegar in a glass of water and drink it down before lunch. It takes me around twenty or thirty minutes to consume it. I definitely recommend it. I don't stop taking care of my gut there.

J U I C E   C L E A N S E

I recommend a one day juice cleanse to all new clients and any client who needs a mental reboot with food. Five juices in one day. It will bring clarity to your weight loss goals and what is needed to achieve them. One day is sufficient to rest your gut. Infuse your body with vitamins and minerals and phytonutrients. The good stuff. You will feel amazing the next day. If you don't, find a new juice place because the juices weren't made from fresh ingredients. Find a local juice company and get to it. Whenever you are off track with food again do another juice cleanse. About that juice cleanses are high in sugar. Nah. What comes from the ground is good for you. It's natural. Healthy. Fruit is not the enemy.

N O U R I S H M E N T

I am the queen of the curbside meal planning consult. In fact I channel it. I give the client a pen and paper and we begin to discuss the time of day that they first feel hungry and go from there. Meal planning is simple. It's about trusting yourself with food. Eating what sounds good to you not what you think you should be eating which is about shame and preparation. I get right to it. The meals and snacks are based on their preferences. I give them two options for each. I am a holistic nutritionist. It goes like this. All food is on the table. Eat the foods that are in your soul. Trust yourself. Build that platform of self love and self discovery. Be good to yourself. Nourish your body with good food. Plan for it. Don't obsess about it. Let everything go that you think you **SHOULD** be doing and begin the process of flow. Combine food in a healthy manner. Your body pulls nutrients out of carbohydrates, protein and fats for cellular energy. Food is fuel for the body. Honor it. Give your body what it needs. I don't recommend counting calories. If it works do it. But most of my clients are busy and this is one more thing to add to an already long list. It's all intuitive for me. Just start making better choices with food. Let go. Your body is beautiful. If you are not a breakfast person. Don't eat breakfast. Pay attention to the cues your body gives you. Give yourself permission to nourish your body when it needs nourishment and that includes before bed. Why should anyone go to bed hungry? Make that snack healthy and light.

How you combine food is very important. Combinations of foods for energy is very important. Your body is a perfect machine. It is efficiently designed to break down food for energy and store it for later. Essential macronutrients are the protein, fats and carbohydrates that your body requires to function period. Food is fuel for the body. Why not give your body what it needs? Not what the latest fast food or cereal commercial force feeds you. I laugh on the rare chance that I watch television and every few minutes there is a fast food or alcohol commercial just in case you were considering wellness. Know these food categories well. Eat what you like. It's not about perfection. Plan ahead. Don't obsess about meal planning. There is such a thing as frozen riced cauliflower. Think combos. Going organic as much as you can is preferred to reduce pesticides and reduce your risk for cancer. When I first started on the Wellness track I chose to go organic with dairy. So eggs and milk. It's a good start. Then I branched out to chicken and turkey burger.

LEAN PROTEIN

Protein is an essential macronutrient. Lean proteins are considered white fish, plain yogurt, beans, chicken or turkey, low-fat cottage cheese, lite tofu, lean beef, powdered peanut butter, pork, egg whites or whole eggs and tempeh. Why is lean protein good for you? Protein is a building block of muscle and aids in cellular repair. For weight loss it has an effect on the hunger hormones leptin and ghrelin by increasing the sensation of fullness and decreasing hunger. It also burns calories at rest. It's a win win. I have so many clients who eat salads for lunch with no lean protein then are ravenous three hours later and binge. Just introducing this concept of adding in goes a long way. Don't worry about portion control because intuitive eating takes care of that. Think when you have food in your mouth. What does it taste like? Slow down. Stop when you are satisfied with it. This process is portion control. Switch up your proteins so you don't get bored.

HEALTHY FATS

Low fat diets don't work. It's the type of fat that is important. Fat is a molecule. The molecule has a surface area. If all aspects of the surface area have fat attached to them then that molecule is saturated with fat. That increases the molecular weight of the molecule. It sinks in the blood stream and can lead to plaque formation over time and heart disease. This is known as saturated fat. Unsaturated fats are when the fat molecule isn't completely bound with fat. They are monounsaturated fats and polyunsaturated fats which are healthy. They are good for your heart and are linked to decreased cholesterol levels. Healthy fats are: avocados, olive oil, nuts, seeds and fatty fish like salmon, albacore tuna. Make sure you get at least two servings of this category daily.

HEALTHY CARBS

This is such a loaded category. There is a lot of misinformation about this group. Your brain uses this category for fuel. There is nothing wrong with this group. I do a lot of reprogramming with my clients regarding healthy carbs. The sugar content is just fine. It's the fiber and protein content that is lights out about this group. There is nothing wrong with apples or bananas. What comes from the ground is good for you. Purists argue that fruit has too much sugar. We need this group. I believe restricting this group outright leads to binge eating. Healthy carbs are: fruit, vegetables, beans, sweet potatoes, red potatoes and whole grains (whole wheat bread, oatmeal, brown rice, quinoa, low carb tortilla) The whole grains are the outlier. Figure out how often you can expose yourself to this group and lose or maintain your weight. The carb content is high. I am fifty eight and I rarely eat any whole grains because I don't feel energized when I do and my belly gets bloated which is inflammation.

SNACKS

Fitness trainers encourage eating every two hours. I don't. If you are training for a competition then go for it. Most of my clients are too busy to do this. If it works go for it but I am into consistency and intuitive eating. Eat when you are hungry and stop when you are satisfied. Snack in between meals if you feel like it or if your energy levels drop. Choose snacks that are from the three categories: lean protein, healthy fats and healthy carbs. I eat lot of dry roasted, lightly salted almonds or apples or plain yogurt with berries. 2 slices or low sodium deli turkey is an option as is 1 Tbsp. of peanut or almond butter with a rice cake. Boiled eggs. String cheese. 2 Tbsp. Hummus with vegetables.

H Y D R A T I O N

While we still have fresh water on this planet hydrate yourself. If your mouth is dry you are dehydrated. Water has so many benefits and is associated with weight loss. Clients ask me all the time how much water to drink. If they have to ask me this question they aren't drinking enough.

Water is critical for the human body. Our bodies are sixty percent water. So if our bodies are sixty percent water it must be important, right? Just drink it. Keep drinking it. It's the 8 X 8 rule. Eight 8-ounce glasses of water or 2 liters. Push it. Keep pushing it.

C A L O R I E   C O U N T I N G

Not a fan of calorie counting. Again I am into consistency and intuitive eating. Your body is a perfect machine. If you are aligned with your body, mind and soul and eat when you are hungry and stop when you are full calorie counting is not needed. During the initial client interview before I even say the words the client beats me to it, "I'm not eating enough or I'm eating too much at the wrong time". Bingo. Intuitive. There are a lot of calorie counting platforms. They take time out of a busy day that you could be living your life instead of counting it. When I first started the business I was into MyFitnessPal. Then I realized that it wasn't sustainable. I should say that when clients are totally off track I recommend a juice cleanse and a two day or one day MyFitnessPal inputting session. My knock on MyFitnessPal is that it has the option of asking whether you want to lose 1 or 2 pounds per week. Of course you opt for the 2 pound loss and this tanks your calories. They are too low and the body will store fat instead of lose it and your metabolism will slow down if the calorie content is too low by about five hundred calories.

Sample Meal Plan for Kelsey

7:15 am Breakfast

Option #1	Option #2
2 eggs	½ c Berries
1c Spinach or greens	1 scoop Collagen Peptide
½ Red bell pepper diced	1 tsp Matcha Powder
Sliced mushrooms	1 c Coconut or AlmondMilk
½ Avocado	½ Avocado
1 slice whole wheat toast	Start pushing water
1 tsp. Butter	
Start pushing water	

Prior to lunch: 1 Tbsp. Of Apple Cider Vinegar in 4 -8 oz of water

12-1 pm Lunch MEAL PREP MEAL PREP MEAL PREP MEAL PREP MEAL PREP MEAL PREP

Options #1	Option #2
Layer Bowl	1 Low carb tortilla
1st layer greens	3 oz shredded chicken or
2nd layer ½ c beans	any kind of beef or turkey burger or fish
½ c diced tomatoes	½ c diced tomatoes
½ c diced cucumbers	Shredded lettuce
3 oz turkey burger seasoned	¼ c cheese
Primal Kitchen Balsamic Vinaigrette	2 Tbsp.¼ c light sour cream

6-7 pm Dinner Meal Plan Meal Plan Meal Plan Meal Plan Meal Plan Meal Plan Meal Plan

Option #1
2 Baked Chicken thighs
Sheet pan cauliflower sliced
Drizzle with olive oil
Baked at 425 for 20 minutes
Green salad
Balsamic vinaigrette 2 Tbsp.

Option #2
3 Turkey Meatballs
1 c whole wheat pasta
or chickpea pasta or
Zucchini noodles
1 Tbsp pesto sauce

M O V E   Y O U R   B O D Y

There is a reason why you have muscles, tendons and ligaments. Move your body. You don't need a gym membership. But you do need to start moving your body. Find an exercise that interests you. Because chances are you will stick to it. Then try another exercise or class that you are interested in. Thirty minutes of exercise is enough to prolong your life span. Imagine that. Your body digs exercise. It increases serotonin levels in the brain. The feel good neurotransmitter. Do it four to five times a week. I am an exercise junkie. At first I walked on my lunch break for an hour five times a week. That preceded a thirty pound weight loss six months later. Then came the treadmill. Then running outside. Then an elliptical. Then yoga and spin and weights and kickboxing and a couple of half marathons, hiking, biking. I love it all. If you are going to own a weight loss center you'd better be in really good shape. If you are going to be a good human and good to your body you'd better be in really good shape. Go outside and exercise. **CARDIO** is important. Getting your heart rate up for 25 – 30 minutes will burn fat. Push yourself. Cardio burns calories and fat and is also a work out for the strongest muscle in your body, your heart. Pace yourself. Jog, ride a bike, spin, fast walk, take a body pump class or boot camp and or swim. Cardio twice a week is great! I don't believe you can achieve your weight loss goals unless you exercise and get in cardio two to three times a week. Exercise is good for the soul.

M E A L   P L A N N I N G

This is it. Planning for nourishment is important. I encourage my clients to perform a mental snapshot at night projecting ahead for the next day. Three days of meal planning is what I recommend. Keep it simple! Eat foods that you like. Remember that store bought food is processed and high in sodium and chemicals for preservation. Taking the time to put a quick meal together is power. It is self care. It is self love. It is simple. Keep in mind that food is energy. Your combination choices are lean protein, healthy fat and healthy carbs. I love food in bowls. I layer greens, beans, turkey burger, cucumber, tomatoes and celery with Balsamic Vinaigrette and that is lunch! If you are a busy mom then it takes more work. But healthy, quick meal recipes are everywhere. Meal planning for lunch is what I focus on and not skipping dinner. Again it is a nourishment issue. You are worthy of nourishing your body, mind and soul with food.

FOUR

THE FIRE OF TRANSFORMATION

When I first started this book I was just beginning my healing journey. I began to do the inside work of letting go of what no longer served my highest good. Breaking down the barriers that surrounded my heart. Hypnotherapy opened so many windows into my subconscious mind. The healing of my soul was and is so necessary. I began to walk through the fire of transformation. Shed myself. Transform as a business owner and a woman. I fear nothing. I continue to step through portals of transformation. I am not the person I was three months ago. If you have read this book you get it. That we never stop learning about ourselves. That weight loss is transformation. What does your weight symbolize? A client who started with me when she was a teenager returned last week. She is now twenty seven. A business owner. In love. Engaged. Super happy except for her weight. I asked her, "What does your weight loss symbolize?" She replied, "I was always the pretty fat girl in high school. It was okay that I was fat because I was pretty. I was accepted. People would say it doesn't matter that you are fat because you are so pretty." The next question I asked her was, "If you weren't the fat girl then who would you be? This is the finest step for you." She smiled and

33

said, "I love you Deb." I am honored to have written this book and to share it with you. To have deep and meaningful conversations with my clients everyday about self love and weight loss. It is why I came. Why I am here. May your weight loss journey be one of self discovery and transformation and also a beautiful one. You are a miracle. You are so loved. Be good to yourself. AHO.

LETTING GO

COMPASSION

SELF LOVE

SOUL HIGHWAY

WAYNEDYER

THE WELLNESS

INSTITUTE

HYPNOTHERAPY

TRUST

LOVE

PEACE

NAMASTE

ABOUT THE AUTHOR

Debra McCurtain is a Certified Heart Centered Hypnotherapist currently in an advanced training internship at The Wellness Institute in Issaquah Washington. She is a Family Nurse Practitioner and a UCSF graduate. Also a Reiki Level 1 Practitioner receiving training at the Santa Monica Healing Center. She is a certified holistic nutritionist. Her day job is that of a CEO of Soul Nutrition and RocklinWeightLoss. She resides in Roseville California at the moment. She has two gifts from the Universe known as Cala and Josh. She is in a relationship with a woman from Boulder Colorado who is known to wear gold pants and Ray Bans.

Printed in the United States
By Bookmasters